GUINNESS WORLD RECORDS

ACTION PACK

S0-DMY-619

SENSATIONAL SURVIVAL RECORDS

Compiled by Kris Hirschmann and Ryan Herndon

For Guinness World Records:
Laura Barrett, Craig Glenday, and Stuart Claxton

SCHOLASTIC INC.
New York   Toronto   London   Auckland   Sydney
Mexico City   New Delhi   Hong Kong   Buenos Aires

Guinness World Records Limited has a very thorough accreditation system for records verification. However, while every effort is made to ensure accuracy, Guinness World Records Limited cannot be held responsible for any errors contained in this work. Feedback from our readers on any point of accuracy is always welcomed.

© 2006 Guinness World Records Limited, a HIT Entertainment Limited Company.

ISBN 0-439-88009-2

Designed by Michelle Martinez Design, Inc.
Photo Research by Els Rijper
Records from the Archives of Guinness World Records

12 11 10 9 8 7 6 5 4 3 2 1   6 7 8 9 10/0

Printed in China

First printing, September 2006

Visit Guinness World Records at www.guinnessworldrecords.com

Do you have what it takes?

For more than 50 years, Guinness World Records has documented the most amazing record-breakers in every imaginable category. Today, their archives contain more than 40,000 entries.

Some of the most astonishing records involve survival and endurance. This book takes a look at 15 of these jaw-dropping records. Read about the **Youngest *Titanic* Survivor**, the **Greatest Spacecraft Collision**, the **Most Lightning Strikes Survived**, and much more. Then try easy activities that explain the science behind the records. You can even use the nifty survival flashlight that comes with this book. Now *that's* a bright idea!

But wait — there's more! When you're done reading, you can test your memory with a trivia quiz about the sensational survival records featured in this book. So **pay attention**. Not only will you ace the quiz, you'll also be able to dazzle your family and friends with facts about the records. And dazzling people, after all, is what Guinness World Records is all about!

Greatest Spacecraft Collision

Space exploration is exciting, but it is also dangerous — especially if spacecrafts hit each other. The **Greatest Spacecraft Collision** took place on June 25, 1997, during a docking test of *Progress*, an unmanned supply craft, with the Russian space station Mir (above). The crafts collided, leaving Mir with a one-inch hole in its hull. No one was injured, but the station suffered **depressurization** — when the air inside the station leaked out into space. Quick-thinking astronauts sealed off the damaged section so no more air could escape. Over the next few months, the crew fixed everything and brought Mir back to full operation. Astronauts continued to live and work inside Mir until August 27, 1999, when the space station was finally shut down for good.

CHECK IT OUT!

The station's international crew transmitted a "we're okay" message to Moscow's Mission Control Center on July 20, 1997. Below, from left to right are: American astronaut Michael Foale with Russian cosmonauts Alexander Lazutkin and Vasily Tsibliyev.

Did you know?

Scientists deliberately crashed the unmanned Mir into the South Pacific Ocean on March 23, 2001. The station left a trail of fireballs across the sky as it entered Earth's atmosphere.

Take Action

The Great Air Escape

The air inside Mir started to escape into space because of differences in air pressure inside and outside the station. High-pressure air always moves toward areas of lower pressure. So when a hole opened in Mir's hull, the high-pressure air inside the station rushed toward the zero-pressure vacuum outside, a process known as **depressurization**.

See how depressurization works with this simple experiment:

1. Blow up a balloon. Tie it closed.
2. Ask an adult to get a thumb tack. Have him or her poke a hole in the softest part of the balloon's neck.
3. Hold the balloon near your ear. Feel and hear the tiny windstream as the higher-pressured air escapes!

Record 2
Highest Fall Survived
Without a Parachute

The **Highest Fall Survived Without a Parachute** occurred on January 26, 1972. On this day, flight attendant Vesna Vulovic was on Yugoslav Air Flight 364 from Denmark to Croatia. Everything went smoothly until a terrorist bomb exploded during the flight. Five crew members and all 22 passengers were killed. Sheltered inside the airplane's wreckage, Vulovic plummeted 33,333 feet (6.3 miles) before crashing into a snow-covered Czechoslovakian mountain. Rescuers found this sole survivor in a coma with a fractured skull, two broken legs, and three broken vertebrae. But Vulovic eventually made a full recovery (above). She went back to work at the airline company for 18 more years before retiring — and she continued to love flying!

Take Action

Falling Speed

Skydivers plunge miles through the sky on purpose! The difference between these people and Vesna Vulovic is that skydivers carry **parachutes** — large cloth canopies that increase the air resistance of falling objects. When a parachute opens, it slows a person's fall to a reasonable speed and helps them land safely on the ground.

To see how a parachute works:

1. Hold a key ring as high as you can, then drop it. See how fast it falls.
2. Now thread one handle of a plastic grocery bag through the key ring. Tie the bag's handles together. Push the key ring down until it touches the knot.
3. Hold the bag with the hanging key ring as high as you can, then drop it. You'll see right away that the key ring falls more slowly than before! The plastic bag acts as a parachute and keeps the key ring from moving as fast as it would on its own.

Record 3
Most Lightning Strikes Survived

Although the chance of being struck by lightning is small, certain jobs put people at risk. Roy C. Sullivan (not pictured in computer-altered image above) holds the record for **Most Lightning Strikes Survived** — seven, to be exact. The "human lightning conductor" was first struck in 1942 (losing his big toenail), then again in 1969 (lost eyebrows), 1970 (left shoulder seared), 1972 (hair set on fire), 1973 (regrown hair singed and legs seared), 1976 (ankle hurt), and 1977 (stomach and chest burns). Sullivan's job as a park ranger in Virginia kept him outdoors during all kinds of stormy weather. This lifestyle greatly increased Sullivan's exposure to lightning — and his chances of being hit.

Did you know?

In the United States, lightning strikes about one of every 600,000 people each year.

Fast Facts!

Roy C. Sullivan once claimed that he could actually see lightning bolts as they headed toward him.

Take Action

Sight vs. Sound

Lightning and thunder are produced at the same instant. But because light travels faster than sound, you see lightning well before you hear its thunder.

To demonstrate the speed difference between light and sound:

1. Lend your survival flashlight to a friend. Near dusk, ask your friend to walk as far down a straight sidewalk as possible (10 house lengths or even more is best). You must be able to see each other.

2. Signal your friend to begin the experiment. Your friend shines the flashlight toward you while he or she shouts loudly. You'll see the light before you hear the shouting!

Record 4
Longest Time Trapped
in an Elevator

December 28, 1987, started out like any other day for 76-year-old Kively Papajohn of Cyprus. Papajohn didn't have a clue that this was the day she would make her mark in the record books for surviving the **Longest Time Trapped in an Elevator**! Returning home from grocery shopping, Papajohn found herself in trouble when her elevator suddenly stopped working. The elevator was so small that Papajohn couldn't even lie down. So she stood in the dark box until she was finally rescued on January 2, 1988 — six long days later. During her ordeal, Papajohn survived by rationing out and nibbling on her groceries: bread, fruit, and tomatoes.

Take Action

Night Vision

People see differently in light and dark conditions. When it's bright, inner-eye receptors called **cones** gather light information. When it's dark, extra-sensitive receptors called **rods** take over. In a completely dark place, like a broken elevator, it takes about 30 minutes for the rods to reach maximum power. Once they do, they can detect even the smallest glimmer of light.

See night vision at work!

1. Tape a piece of black paper over the light end of your survival flashlight. Make sure the light is completely covered. Then ask a grown-up to poke a pinhole in the paper.
2. Go into the darkest place in your house (such as a closet with a door you can close, or a bathroom with no windows). Right away, shine the flashlight around. You can barely see the tiny pinhole of light.
3. Turn off the flashlight and wait five minutes, then try again. Your night vision will have adjusted by now and you'll see how the light blazes brightly!

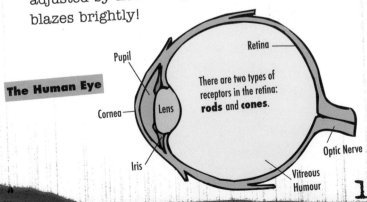

The Human Eye

Pupil

Retina

Cornea

Lens

There are two types of receptors in the retina: **rods** and **cones**.

Iris

Optic Nerve

Vitreous Humour

Longest Post-Earthquake Survival by a Cat

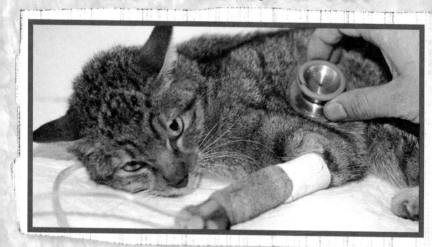

xperts believe that survivors trapped inside collapsed buildings have little chance of being rescued after 48 hours have passed. But one lucky cat survived an incredible *80 days* after a devastating earthquake hit Taiwan. The quake, which measured between 7.3 and 7.6 on the Richter scale, struck on September 21, 1999. More than 2,000 aftershocks (minor earthquakes) rocked Taiwan over the next two days. An estimated 2,400 people did not survive. On December 9, 1999, searchers found a cat pinned beneath a large message board inside a house in the city of Taichung. The animal was starving, dehydrated, and barely breathing — but it was alive. A TV reporter rushed the cat to a veterinary hospital, where it was warmed and fed (above). After experiencing the **Longest Post-Earthquake Survival by a Cat**, this fortunate feline made a full recovery.

Take Action

Bright Eyes

Cat eyes contain a reflective layer named the **tapetum lucidum** (or tapetum, for short). The tapetum makes light beams bounce around inside the cat's eye, which improves night vision. Sometimes the tapetum also reflects light back *out* of the eye. That's why cats' eyes sometimes seem to glow in the dark.

You could use the tapetum to find a trapped cat! Here's how:

1. Coax a cat into a dark place, like under a bed. Imagine it's buried under a pile of rubble and you must find it.
2. Hold your flashlight near your face. Turn it on and move the light beam around. When the beam gets near the cat's face, the eyes will start to glow!

Don't have a cat? You can still check out an animal's night vision. Talk with a parent about going together on a nature walk after sunset — and take along your survival flashlight. Many animals, including rabbits, deer, raccoons, and bullfrogs, have reflective eyes. Use your flashlight and see who glows back at you!

Record 6
Youngest *Titanic* Survivor

Elizabeth Gladys "Millvina" Dean was born on February 2, 1912. When baby Millvina was just nine weeks old, the Dean family set sail on the "unsinkable" R.M.S. *Titanic.* The family dreamed of running a tobacco shop in America. But their dream was shattered on the night of April 14–15 when the *Titanic* hit an iceberg and began sinking. Millvina's father, Bertram, managed to get his wife, young son, and newborn daughter into a lifeboat. Bertram himself went down with the ship (illustration, opposite page) — but thanks to his heroic efforts, the rest of the Dean family were among the 706 survivors from the ship's 2,223 passengers. Millvina Dean did not remember becoming the Youngest *Titanic* Survivor. But today, at age 94, she speaks about her life's experiences at historical conventions around the world (bottom, opposite page).

CHECK IT OUT!

Researchers found the wreck of the *Titanic* on September 1, 1985. The wreck lies 2 miles below the sea surface, about 375 miles southeast of Newfoundland.

Millvina Dean did not learn about her incredible *Titanic* experience until she was eight years old.

MILLVINA CLOSE

Take Action

Colder than Ice

On the night the *Titanic* went down, scientists estimate that the water temperature was 28° Fahrenheit. That's *below* freezing (32°F)! The water didn't turn into ice because it contained salt, which actually lowers the freezing temperature of water.

To see this effect for yourself:

1. In a disposable cup, combine 1 small spoonful of salt and 3 small spoonfuls of water. Stir until the salt dissolves.
2. Into another disposable cup, put 4 small spoonfuls of regular water.
3. Label the cups so you can remember which is which. Put both cups into the freezer. Check them regularly. Which cup of water freezes first?

Longest Lifeboat Journey

In 1914, Sir Ernest Shackleton headed for Antarctica with a 28-man crew. He never made it to his destination. By early 1915, Shackleton's ship, the *Endurance*, was frozen fast in Antarctic sea ice. Everyone piled into three lifeboats and set course for Elephant Island, about 100 miles to the north. After arriving, Shackleton and five crew members then traveled in the largest lifeboat to a whaling station on South Georgia Island, 800 miles away (above). The crew arrived on May 19, 1916, after a 17-day trip — the **Longest Lifeboat Journey** ever. Ten days later, they reached the whaling station on foot. Shackleton told the people there about the men trapped on Elephant Island. The entire crew was eventually rescued, making this story one of history's most incredible survival tales.

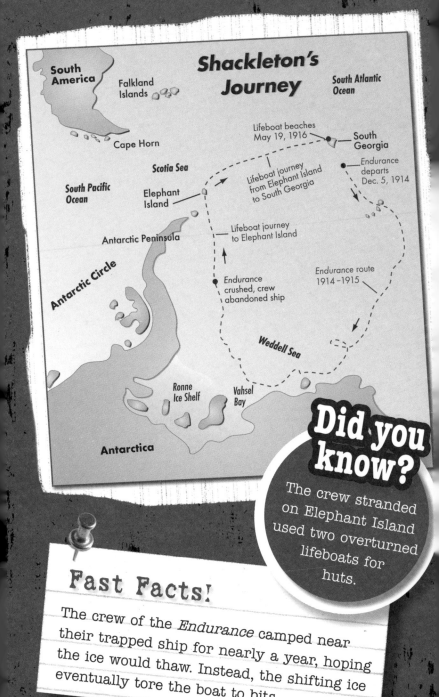

Shackleton's Journey

South America

South Atlantic Ocean

Falkland Islands

Lifeboat beaches May 19, 1916

South Georgia

Cape Horn

Endurance departs Dec. 5, 1914

Scotia Sea

Lifeboat journey from Elephant Island to South Georgia

South Pacific Ocean

Elephant Island

Lifeboat journey to Elephant Island

Antarctic Peninsula

Endurance route 1914–1915

Antarctic Circle

Endurance crushed, crew abandoned ship

Weddell Sea

Ronne Ice Shelf

Vahsel Bay

Antarctica

Did you know?

The crew stranded on Elephant Island used two overturned lifeboats for huts.

Fast Facts!

The crew of the *Endurance* camped near their trapped ship for nearly a year, hoping the ice would thaw. Instead, the shifting ice eventually tore the boat to bits.

Take Action

Changing Direction

Shackleton and his crew found their way partly with the help of a compass. Compasses contain metal pointers that are pulled by Earth's magnetic fields. Since compasses always point north, these handy instruments are reliable navigation tools.

To make your own compass:

1. With a permanent marker, color one end of a small paper clip.
2. Stroke the paper clip with a magnet about 50 times. Stroke in the same direction each time, moving from the uncolored end to the colored end.
3. Fill a cup with water all the way to the brim.
4. Set the paper clip on a flat piece of cork or anything else that floats. Set everything on the water's surface. Watch as your paper clip swings around to point north — *every time!*

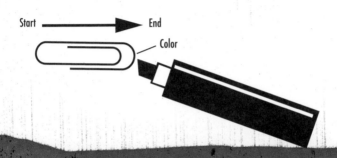

During World War II, a young Chinese man named Poon Lim was a steward aboard the British Merchant Navy's S.S. *Ben Lomond*. A German U-boat torpedoed the ship near Brazil on November 23, 1942. Lim escaped by climbing onto an empty life raft, but its limited supplies would not be enough to keep him alive. Undaunted, the resourceful castaway caught fish with hooks he had made from nails and flashlight parts. At one point he even managed to grab and eat a sea bird. Lim scraped by until April 5, 1943, when a fishing boat finally rescued him. He had survived for an amazing 133 days — the **Longest Time Adrift at Sea Alone**. The photograph (above) shows Poon Lim in an historical reenactment of his journey.

Take Action

Morse Code

If Poon Lim had a working flashlight, he could have communicated with distant ships in Morse code! This famous code combines long and short bursts of light or sound to represent letters. Long flashes (dash) last 3 times longer than short flashes (dot). The sender transmits at a reasonable speed to the receiver, who then translates the bursts into words.

Use the chart below to spell out Morse code messages with your survival flashlight.

.- A	--. G	-- M	... S	-.-- Y
-... B	.... H	-. N	- T	--.. Z
-.-. C	.. I	--- O	..- U	
-.. D	.--- J	.--. P	...- V	
. E	-.- K	--.- Q	.-- W	
..-. F	.-.. L	.-. R	-..- X	

KEY

. = short flash
- = long flash

Did you know?

Morse code is named after Samuel Morse, the inventor of the electric telegraph.

Record 9
Deepest Underwater
Escape with No Equipment

The human body was never meant to survive unprotected far below the sea surface. Richard A. Slater (opposite page) knows this fact first-hand as the record-holder for the **Deepest Underwater Escape with No Equipment**. On September 28, 1970, Slater was operating a small submarine called the *Nekton Beta*, trying to raise a sunken powerboat off the California coast. During the operation, the powerboat accidentally rammed the *Beta*, shattering an observation port and stunning Slater. The damaged craft sank to the bottom of the sea, 225 feet below, filling with water (top, opposite page). Semiconscious, Slater managed to push open the sub's hatch and launch himself into open water. He struggled to the ocean surface, where he was quickly picked up and rushed to shore — alive!

CHECK IT OUT!

The **Deepest Diving Submersible in Service** is the *Shinkai 6500*, a Japanese research craft. This three-person vessel can reach a depth of more than 21,000 feet.

Did you know?

The depth limit for safe recreational diving is considered to be 130 feet.

Take Action

Under Pressure

Scientists use units called **atmospheres** to measure air and water pressure. The pressure at sea level is exactly one atmosphere. As you travel down into the ocean, the pressure increases at a rate of one atmosphere per 33 feet. So the pressure on a submarine 33 feet below the sea surface is two atmospheres. The pressure at 66 feet is three atmospheres, and so on.

Figure it out:

Richard Slater escaped from a depth of 225 feet. About how many atmospheres of pressure did he experience at the moment of escape?

Answer: Slater experienced 7.8 atmospheres — nearly 8 times the pressure at sea level! Unfortunately, the intense pressure ruptured Slater's eardrums.

The English Channel is a part of the Atlantic Ocean that separates France and England. Measuring 21 miles at its narrowest point, the Channel is cold, tide swept, and choppy. Crossing it is the ultimate challenge for any swimmer. The challenge certainly appealed to World Masters Swimming Champion George Brunstad (above), who tackled this monumental task on August 29, 2004 — four days after his seventieth birthday. Brunstad completed the trip from England to France in 15 hours and 59 minutes to become the **Oldest Channel Swimmer**. After setting the world record, Brunstad commented on his experience, "I thought I could make it, but it was pretty darn uncomfortable."

CHECK IT OUT!

There are practically no sharks in the English Channel. So that's at least one thing a Channel swimmer doesn't have to worry about.

England

Dover

Folkestone

Hythe

English Channel

Calais

France

Boulogne

Did you know?

George Brunstad is the uncle of movie star Matt Damon.

Take Action

Tidal Pull

During an English Channel swim, tidal forces pull swimmers north and south as they travel. For this reason, the course of a Channel swim looks like a sideways "S" rather than a straight line.

See the effect of tides on the length of a swim:

1. Cut a piece of string just long enough to cover the "S" curve between points A and B.
2. Hold one end of the string against point A. Stretch the string out straight. It goes far past point B. You can see that Channel swimmers actually swim much farther than the official Channel width of 21 miles!

A

B

Longest-Ever Running Race

The **Longest-Ever Running Race** was held from March 31 to June 17, 1929. The 3,635-mile course connected New York City and Los Angeles, California. This astonishing distance was no problem for Finnish-born Johnny Salo (above, left), who won the race after 79 days on the road. Salo's elapsed time of 525 hours, 57 minutes, and 20 seconds beat second-place Pietro "Peter" Gavuzzi (above, right) — by 2 minutes and 47 seconds! This was a closer finish than the numbers suggest. At the start of the last day, Gavuzzi was the clear leader. But race officials made a mistake that gave Salo a head start of five to six minutes. Without this mistake, Gavuzzi would have taken home the record.

Take Action

Speed Racer

In the final portion of the 1929 race, winner Johnny Salo raised the pace to a blistering 10.5 miles per hour. That's roughly 19.5 seconds per 100 yards.

Do you think you can equal Salo's pace?

1. Find a football field. Stand on one of the goal lines.
2. Get a friend to time you. Run to the opposite goal line (which is exactly 100 yards away) as fast as you can. Did you beat 20 seconds?

Did you know?

Kenyan Paul Tergat completed the **Fastest Marathon** (26.2 miles) **Ever Run** in 2 hours, 4 minutes, 55 seconds. That averages out to about 16.35 seconds per 100 yards.

Record 12
Longest Duration
Balancing on One Foot

The record for the **Longest Duration Balancing on One Foot** is held by Sri Lankan-born Arulanantham Suresh Joachim (above). Between May 22 and 25, 1997, Joachim balanced on one foot for 76 hours and 40 minutes. That's more than three entire days! Joachim's feat seems even more incredible if you consider that most people can't balance on one foot for even a single minute. The trick, say some karate experts, is to relax the weight-bearing foot completely, since a twitching foot makes the whole body unstable. Going barefoot supposedly makes you more aware of your feet and helps you to stay still. Good overall muscle tone also helps in tests of endurance.

Take Action

Endurance Test

How close can you come to breaking Joachim's record? Try it and see! Just remember the rules of Guinness World Records for this attempt: The nonsupporting foot cannot be rested on the standing foot, and no alternative object can be used for support or balance.

Here's what you do:

1. Clear your schedule. Joachim lasted for three and a half days, so you'll need even more time to set a new record.
2. Stand on one foot. And stand, and stand, and stand. Time yourself and have a friend check on you. How long did you keep your second foot off the floor?

Did you know?

Human balance is controlled by the semicircular canal, located inside the inner ear structure.

Fast Facts!

Suresh Joachim has broken dozens of Guinness World Records, including the **Longest Time Spent Watching TV** (69 hours, 48 minutes), **Longest Distance Carrying a 10-Pound Brick** (78.7121 miles), and **Longest Drumming Marathon** (84 hours).

Youngest Person to Trek to the South Pole

Trekking guide Matty McNair had twice visited the South Pole by age 53. She turned her third trip into a family vacation! Matty, along with son Eric McNair-Landry (age 20), daughter Sarah Ann McNair-Landry (age 18), and a British couple, set out on skis on November 1, 2004. They towed heavy sleds piled with fuel, equipment, and food. For weeks the team slogged through whipping winds and temperatures that plunged to −49 degrees Fahrenheit. After traveling 683 miles, the group arrived safely at the South Pole Marker (above), earning Sarah the record as the **Youngest Person to Trek to the South Pole**. Sarah claims she was never nervous about making the trip. "If you start thinking about the risks, you would be stuck inside all the time," she says.

Take Action

Blinding Sight

Polar trekkers wear sunglasses to protect themselves from **snowblindness**, or sunburn of the eyeballs. Snowblindness occurs when the ground reflects sunlight into people's eyes. The color white reflects more light than any other color, so snowblindness is especially common near the Earth's poles.

See how white will reflect light:

1. Get a piece of white paper, a piece of black paper, and your survival flashlight. Find a dark place, such as a closet.
2. Hold the black paper about a foot from any wall. Shine your flashlight onto the wall-facing side of the paper. Notice the amount of light reflected onto the wall.
3. Repeat Step 2 with the white paper. Much more light bounces onto the wall!

Did you know?

In polar-expedition lingo, **trekking** means traveling without the use of dogs or motorized vehicles.

First Solo Ascent of Mount Everest

Standing 29,028 feet tall, Mount Everest is the **Highest Mountain** (opposite page). Only about 2,500 people have ever stood on Everest's summit. And of these climbers, just one — Reinhold Messner (top, opposite page) — has ever done it alone. Messner first reached Everest's summit on May 8, 1978, with another climber, Peter Habeler, and set the record for **First Ascent of Mount Everest Without Oxygen**. On August 20, 1980, Messner was determined to set another daring and dangerous record — climbing the mountain without a partner. His combination of skill, brains, and luck helped Messner complete the **First Solo Ascent of Mount Everest**. Today, the mountain is covered with people during climbing season, so it is unlikely that anyone will ever have the opportunity to break Messner's record.

CHECK IT OUT!

Reinhold Messner claims that he has seen the **yeti** (also known as the abominable snowman) three times while climbing in the Himalayas. No photographic proof exists (right, an actor wears a yeti costume).

Did you know?

Nearly 200 people have died while trying to climb Mount Everest.

Take Action

Sky High

Before modern measuring technologies were invented, people used primitive methods to measure the height of mountains and trees.

You can make a tree-measuring device:

1. Assemble a protractor, a drinking straw, a piece of string, and a metal washer as shown. Use tape as necessary to hold things together.
2. Use a marker to draw a dark line along the 45° line on the protractor.
3. Sight the top of any tree through the drinking straw. Move backward or forward, keeping the treetop in sight, until the string hangs exactly along the 45° line on the protractor.
4. Mark the place where you are standing. Then measure the distance from your spot to the tree trunk. This distance, plus your own height, equals the height of the tree. (For example, if you are 4 feet tall and you are standing 20 feet from the tree trunk, the tree is about 24 feet tall.)

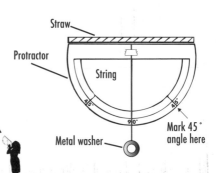

Straw

Protractor

String

45°   45°

90°

Mark 45° angle here

Metal washer

GUINNESS WORLD RECORDS™

In 1800, a St. Bernard puppy named Barry was born in a high, storm-swept region of the Swiss Alps. This puppy was destined to earn a spot in the record books as the **Most Celebrated Canine Rescuer** (not pictured). Monks trained Barry to find travelers who had lost their way in the snow. Barry was a natural at this task. During his 12-year career, Barry found and saved at least 40 people — more than any other St. Bernard rescuer before or since. Today, a monument in memory of Barry and his incredible achievements stands guard at the entrance of a famous pet cemetery in Paris, France.

Take Action

Blanket of Snow

Snow is a good insulator, which means it traps warmth. It does this because it is made mostly (up to 90 percent) of trapped air — and air does not transfer heat well. This property is helpful to buried avalanche victims. No matter how cold the open air gets, the snow will never dip below 32° Fahrenheit.

To see how much air is trapped in snow:

1. Get a family-size loaf of Wonder Bread (Wonder Bread has an air/solid ratio similar to snow.) Remove the loaf from its bag.
2. Squash the entire loaf into the smallest possible ball. Surprisingly little bread remains when the air is removed!

Did you know?

St. Bernard dogs have saved more than 2,000 travelers in Switzerland.

Check Your
FACTS!

How **good** is your memory?

You've read the records and done the activities. Now turn the page and answer 30 trivia questions about the information in this book. When you're done, check your answers on page 44.

TRIVIA

1 Greatest Spacecraft Collision

1. What country operated the space station Mir?
2. **True or false?** Low-pressure air moves toward areas of higher pressure.

2 Highest Fall Survived Without a Parachute

1. What caused Yugoslav Air Flight 364 to crash?
2. **True or false?** Vesna Vulovic recovered fully from her record-breaking fall.

3 Most Lightning Strikes Survived

1. What was the profession of Roy C. Sullivan, the "human lightning conductor"?
2. Which travels faster: light or sound?

4 Longest Time Trapped in an Elevator

1. What food did Kively Papajohn eat while she was trapped in an elevator?
2. Which sensors in the human eye are responsible for night vision: rods or cones?

5 Longest Post-Earthquake Survival by a Cat

1. In what country did the longest post-earthquake-surviving cat live?
2. Which organ in certain animals contains a light-reflecting structure named the *tapetum lucidum*?

6 Youngest *Titanic* Survivor

1. Why did the *Titanic* sink?
2. How many Dean family members survived the sinking of the *Titanic*?

7 Longest Lifeboat Journey

1. Where was Sir Ernest Shackleton's ship, the *Endurance*, originally headed?
2. What makes a compass point north?

8 Longest Time Adrift at Sea Alone

1. What war was going on during Poon Lim's record-breaking ordeal?

2. One well-known Morse code message is:
... - - - ... (dot dot dot / dash dash dash / dot dot dot) —
what does it stand for?

9 Deepest Underwater Escape with No Equipment
1. What was the name of the submarine from which Richard A. Slater escaped?
2. What units are used to measure air and water pressure?

10 Oldest Channel Swimmer
1. How old was George Brunstad when he swam across the English Channel?
2. Which sideways letter resembles the path of an English Channel swimmer?

11 Longest-Ever Running Race
1. What two cities were the start and end points of the longest-ever running race?
2. In what year was the longest-ever running race held?

12 Longest Duration Balancing on One Foot
1. **True or false?** Record-breaker Suresh Joachim held a long pole to help him balance on one foot.
2. Where is the semicircular canal located inside the human body?

13 Youngest Person to Trek to the South Pole
1. What mode of travel did Sarah Ann McNair-Landry use to reach the South Pole?
2. What color reflects the most sunlight?

14 First Solo Ascent of Mount Everest
1. About how many people have stood atop Mount Everest?
2. How tall is Mount Everest?
   A. 9,035 feet   **B.** 19,035 feet   **C.** 29,028 feet

15 Most Celebrated Canine Rescuer
1. What mountainous area is famous for its history of St. Bernard rescue dogs?
2. How many travelers were saved by Barry the St. Bernard?

TRIVIA
answers

Record 1
1. Russia operated the space station Mir.
2. (False) High-pressure air moves toward areas of lower pressure.

Record 2
1. A terrorist bomb caused Yugoslav Air Flight 364 to crash.
2. (True) Vesna Vulovic made a complete recovery.

Record 3
1. Roy C. Sullivan was a park ranger.
2. Light travels much faster than sound.

Record 4
1. Kively Papajohn ate her groceries of bread, fruit, and tomatoes.
2. Rods are responsible for human night vision.

Record 5
1. The cat lived in Taiwan.
2. The eyes of certain animals contain the *tapetum lucidum*.

Record 6
1. The *Titanic* sank because it ran into an iceberg.
2. Three Dean family members survived the *Titanic* sinking.

Record 7
1. The *Endurance* was heading for Antarctica.
2. Earth's magnetic field pulls the compass metal north.

Record 8
1. Poon Lim's journey occurred during World War II.
2. The signal: ... --- ... (dot dot dot / dash dash dash / dot dot dot) stands for SOS, a distress call sent out by ships in trouble.

Record 9
1. Richard A. Slater escaped from a submarine named *Nekton Beta*.
2. Units called atmospheres measure air and water pressure.

Record 10
1. George Brunstad was 70 years old when he swam across the English Channel.
2. The path of an English Channel swimmer resembles the letter *S*.

Record 11
1. The longest-ever running race started in New York City and ended in Los Angeles, CA.
2. The longest-ever running race was held in 1929.

Record 12
1. (False) According to the rules, no object can be used for support or balance.
2. The human inner ear structure contains the semicircular canal.

Record 13
1. Sarah Ann McNair-Landry skied to the South Pole.
2. White reflects more light than any other color.

Record 14
1. About 2,500 climbers have reached Mount Everest's summit.
2. (C.) Mount Everest is 29,028 feet tall.

Record 15
1. The Swiss Alps are famous for its history of raising St. Bernard rescue dogs.
2. A St. Bernard named Barry rescued at least 40 travelers.

Congratulations! You survived!

Our book is nearly over — but your record-breaking experience doesn't have to be. You can explore more sensational facts and feats among the online archives (www.guinnessworldrecords.com) and within the pages of *Guinness World Records* at your local library or bookstore. You're guaranteed to find thousands of amazing and inspiring records set by people and animals living around the globe.

If reading about records isn't enough, why not become a record-breaker yourself? Check out the official guidelines on page 47 and **go for it**. Maybe *your* name will appear in the next edition of the record books!

Photo Credits

How to be a Record-Breaker

Message from the Keeper of the Records:

Record-breakers are the ultimate in one way or another — the youngest, the oldest, the tallest, the smallest. So how do you get to be a record-breaker? Follow these important steps:

1. Before you attempt your record, check with us to make sure your record is suitable and safe. Get your parents' permission. Next, contact one of our officials by using the record application form at *www.guinnessworldrecords.com*.

2. Tell us about your idea. Give us as much information as you can, including what the record is, when you want to attempt it, where you'll be doing it, and other relevant information.

   a) We will tell you if a record already exists, what safety guidelines you must follow during your attempt to break that record, and what evidence we need as proof that you completed your attempt.

   b) If your idea is a brand-new record nobody has set yet, we need to make sure it meets our requirements. If it does, then we'll write official rules and safety guidelines specific to that record idea and make sure all attempts are made in the same way.

3. Whether it is a new or existing record, we will send you the guidelines for your selected record. Once you receive these, you can make your attempt at any time. You do not need a Guinness World Record official at your attempt. But you do need to gather evidence. Find out more about the kind of evidence we need to see by visiting our website.

4. Think you've already set or broken a record? Put all of your evidence as specified by the guidelines in an envelope and mail it to us at Guinness World Records.

5. Our officials will investigate your claim fully — a process that can take a few weeks, depending on the number of claims we've received and how complex your record is.

6. If you're successful, you will receive an official certificate that says you are now a Guinness World Record-holder!

Need more info? Check out the Kids' Zone on *www.guinnessworldrecords.com/kidszone* for lots more hints, tips, and top record ideas that you can try at home or at school. Good luck!

Break a record and one day you could appear in the **Guinness World Records** book! Here's what you'll find in the 2007 edition of the world's best-selling annual...

* Over 1,500 new amazing, **mind-blowing records**

* Exclusive celebrity **interviews**

* Incredible **new photos**

* All-new **giant gatefold** feature sections

* More ways than ever to **get your name in the book**!

GUINNESS WORLD RECORDS 2007

Your record here!

ON SALE AUGUST 2006!